ODUNTAN ADEBOGA

LIFE IS BEAUTIFUL

Living within the Confines of Purpose

LIFE IS BEAUTIFUL

LIFE IS BEAUTIFUL

LIVING WITHIN THE CONFINES OF PURPOSE

ODUNTAN ADEBUGA

ISBN: 9798848005653

For information contact Odutan Adebuga at odun1108@gmail.com

To all children of God; redeemed and justified, who have strong desires to live a purpose-driven and impactful life.

CONTENTS

ACKNOWLEDGMENTS

Unto the King eternal, immortal, invisible, the only wise God, be honour and glory for ever and ever Amen.
(1 Timothy 1:17)

My highest praise to God who freely gave His grace, to Jesus Christ, the Saviour of mankind who delivered us from the power of darkness and translated us to the Kingdom of God and for granting us free access to God by the Holy Ghost.

I will forever be grateful to my darling wife, Abosede Adebuga for the support and encouragement I received from her while writing this book. Lots of appreciation for her prayers that kept me going in spite of obstacles encountered on my life journey. My gratitude also goes to my brothers and sisters whose support contributed to the successful publication of the book. I am grateful.

Special appreciation to Pastor Joseph Kolawole Ola, an author of several titles, Editor, Restoration Today Daily Devotional, who pastors at The Apostolic Church Liverpool, Merseyside in the United Kingdom and Phillip Akindamola Akinyoola, an ardent entrepreneur for editing the manuscript and making useful observations, corrections and contributions to the book despite their busy schedule. I owe you both a debt of gratitude - your insight and creativity enhanced the book. The good Lord will bless you and load you with benefits of all kinds.

Israel Adebayo Fadahunsi, you are a brother indeed, a twin brother from another mother. Your support towards the production of this book is second to none. You really displayed brotherly love, always responding to my calls at any point in time. You are blessed.

I also want to appreciate a man of God, a father indeed, Pastor Samuel A. Ogunjobi, an Area Superintendent in The Apostolic Church Nigeria, LAWNA Territory for his fatherly care, love and support for me and my family.

PREFACE

Life is a precious gift given to man by God, as all that God created was adjudged beautiful. God also loaded man with extended potentials to affect his world. God created man in His own image purposely to continue creation. Hence, He has given man all that pertains to life and godliness and maintains an active line of communication through the Holy Spirit who reveals the unknown but needed and sure path to achieving one's life purpose.

You may be thinking that your coming into this world is just for coming sake, where you come and return at the end of the day without achieving any specific purpose. Unless you discover your specific purpose you will become irrelevant to the purpose why you are created.

Human brilliance will in the end amount to mere counting days, years, children, houses, cars and eventually lead nowhere until such a life discovers God's purpose and work towards fulfilling it. Success is a measure of standard on a particular specification of an assignment. Thus, until you pursue the achievement of your life's purpose with God's specification, your results cannot amount to a beautiful life.

Our only wise God has embedded in His creation and within your environment all that constitute the needed ingredients to fulfil your purpose. So life can be beautiful even in its harsh terrain when man walks in line with his life-purpose and life can be marred in its comfortable terrain when man walks outside of his purpose. Therefore, my key message to you is that you can make your life beautiful in any place you find yourself. Please turn the few pages of this book to discover how you can.

I pray that as you read this book, God will open your eyes to see the revelations you need, enlighten you on your life's purpose and strengthen you for the race and fire you up to run tirelessly until you conform to His image and achieve all He has purposed for your life.

Your guiding light is your God-given purpose. You cannot thrive until you discover it and you cannot fail to thrive as long as you align yourself with it.

~

You made all the delicate, inner parts of my body and knit me together in my mother's womb. Thank you for making me so wonderfully complex! Your workmanship is marvelous—how well I know it.

Psalm 139:13-14 (NLT)

CHAPTER 1

NOTHING JUST HAPPENS

Before I formed you in the womb I knew you, before you were born I set you apart; I appointed you as a prophet to the nations. — **Jeremiah 1:5 (NIV)**

~

As there are no aimless machines, there is no man without a divine purpose and specific assignment.

Everything created in this world is for a purpose —nothing just happens for the sake of happening. There is a purpose for everything made. Manufacturers construct machines for certain purposes. Cars are produced for the movement of men, other creatures and things from one place to another. Houses are built to provide shelter for people.

Telephones are conceptualised and produced for communication and social interaction between two or more people. Books are written for transfer of knowledge and skills in various fields of studies. Everything was designed with a purpose in mind.

Rick Warren wrote in his book, *The Purpose Driven Life*,

> “God never does anything accidentally, and he never makes mistakes. He has a reason for everything He creates.[1]

You did not just happen; there is a certain purpose for your existence. Your coming into this world may not have been planned for by your parents, but God did because He knew everything before your conception and also had the foreknowledge of your purpose in life.

> “. . . *Nothing about me is hidden from you!*
>
> *I was secretly woven together deep in the earth below but with your own eyes, you saw my body being formed.*
>
> *Even before I was born, you had written in your book everything I would do*”
>
> — PSALM 139:14-16 (CEV)

You did not just happen by chance, you have a purpose to fulfil in life and with God's help you will definitely fulfil that purpose. Your purpose is the way God plans to make an impact on the world through you. So until you tap into that purpose you can never be fulfilled in life.

Purpose elevates man out of the ordinary and common class of men and makes him rise above natural limitations. It makes him unique and valuable to the world around him.

The book of Jeremiah 1:5 says

> *"Before I formed you in the womb, I knew you, before you were born I set you apart: I appointed you as a prophet to the nations"* (NIV).

The verse indicates that every man is divinely ordained for a specific purpose. You cannot be indifferent - There is no man without a specific purpose for his life; unless he has not taken time to discover what he is created for.

Therefore, it is not only those that are set aside through anointing that are divinely ordained; every man has been divinely anointed by God for a specific assignment. There are some assignments that are better done by you: every other person that tries to copy it cannot do it as you can because they weren't configured for it as you have been. This infers that only you can do the specific assignments designated to you. If you do not do it, it will not be done by someone else for you. Fulfilling the purpose designated to each of us is absolutely our individual's responsibility. You cannot fulfil mine, I cannot fulfil yours. Each of us has that unique responsibility.

Prophet Isaiah gave a prophecy of what the ministry of Jesus will be cut-out for, he said;

> “*The spirit of the Lord is upon me because the Lord hath anointed me to preach good tidings unto the meek; he hath sent me to bind up the broken hearted, to proclaim liberty to the captives, and the opening of the prison to them that are bound. To proclaim the acceptable year of the Lord, and the day of vengeance of our God, to comfort all that mourn. To appoint unto them that mourn in Zion, to give unto them beauty for ashes, the oil of joy for mourning, the garment of praise for the spirit of heaviness that they might be called trees of righteousness, the planting of the Lord, that he might be glorified*”
>
> — ISAIAH 61:1-3

When Jesus came hundreds of years later, He went to the temple, opened scripture, read it and declared its fulfilment to the congregation. As the Captain of man's salvation, Jesus knew He was not sent for "the righteous" but to save man from sin and destroy the works of darkness. He knew what the purpose of God for His life was and spent the whole of His earthly ministry doing it.

The following scriptures establish the purpose of Jesus to men:

> *The thief comes only to steal and kill and destroy; I have come that they may have life, and have it to the full*
>
> —JOHN 10:10 (NIV)

> *Even as the Son of man came not to be ministered unto, but to minister, and to give his life a ransom for many*
>
> — MATTHEW 20:28

> *. . . For this purpose the Son of God was manifested, that he might destroy the works of the devil*
>
> — 1 JOHN 3:8B

On the way to Damascus, Paul got the divine purpose for his life. He was called to be a minister and a witness of the things he saw and the things that will be revealed to him thereafter; to open the eyes of the Jews and the Gentiles in order to turn them from darkness to light, from the power of Satan to God.

It is tragic to be alive and not to know the reason why. If you do not understand the purpose of your life, you will abuse it. This prioritises the inevitability of figuring out that *one thing* you were born to be, and stop trying to be what you are not. Life is best lived on purpose. When you have a clear purpose in life things seem less complicated, but when you are not living on purpose, life becomes difficult and oppressive.

Your life purpose makes your life significant, shows to you and the rest of the world that your life counts, has meaning and is capable of making the world a better place.

Purpose brings tremendous joy to man, uplifts him to a higher dimension where divine energy is released to make him fulfil his calling. It assigns a specific assignment to him and this assignment is something he likes to do, something that is easy for him, something that brings joy and enthusiasm.

As there are no aimless machines, there is no man without divine purpose and specific assignment. It is only that many have not taken enough time to discover their reason for living.

While some have a specific assignment in the deliverance ministry, some are assigned with the preaching of the gospel, some others with the ministry of songs, and some others with the drama ministry. As some are gifted in architectural drawing, some are gifted in building a structure from the architectural piece. Also someone is wired to design clothes, and another is gifted to style the hair for men and women.

You are not a mistake neither are you a coincidence nor a waste to your generation. You have a specific assignment you are cut-out for. You are a unique blend of gifts and character. You have a special purpose on earth. Discovering that specific purpose and assignment is what makes you find yourself and your life purposeful. It makes life worth living as well as making your world a beautiful place. It gives your life meaning and with this meaning comes significance and hope.

Your guiding light is your God-given purpose. You cannot thrive until you discover it and you cannot fail to thrive as long as you align yourself with it. If you can tune into your purpose and align with it then life will flow much more easily.

People with the highest degree of frustration are the people who have not identified their purpose and specific assignment: they have no fixed purpose as a result, they are lost in life. When people are not absolutely sure of where the Lord is leading them, they become wanderers. They wander around aimlessly with no clue of where they are going and what they are cut-out for. Those who have discovered theirs will always be more productive than those who have not. They function at their peak.

Without discovering why you exist on this planet earth, life will be meaningless, trivial and pointless, and even not worth living. The very thing you will enjoy most and can do best is the thing you are cut-out for. Many who have not discovered their life-purpose jump from one place to the other, without any major achievement. Such people jump into a business because a friend is thriving in such a business. Instead of going in the right direction of their purpose, they are always following others.

In God's plan, not everyone is gifted to own a business, neither is everyone assigned to work as an employee. God has different plans for everyone. If you were engineered to be a Ford truck, you cannot pretend to be a Volkswagen Beetle. So, since you are created by a Superior Being, more powerful than you are and imbued with natural tendencies and gifts in order to contribute those things to positively affect the world, you will do yourself a lot of good by submitting to that particular purpose for which you were created. Maximising and profiting with your gift is your gift back to God. Whether God called you to be a minister of the gospel or a furniture maker or a businessman—it cannot change because God made it so.

Be confident that God has a plan for your life, a specific assignment, a divine call, a path on which He wants to guide you and what you live your life for on planet earth. There are great discoveries but the greatest discovery you could have made is self-discovery, so find yourself. You will find yourself when you discover your purpose.

The assurance is that whatever God has purposed and designed for you will make you live a beautiful and fulfilled life here on planet earth and by conforming to this, you will have impact on the world around you. Just believe in your purpose.

It is one thing to discover purpose, another thing is to believe that you can actually fulfil that purpose and have an impact on the world around you. Even if those around you do not believe the level of impact you can achieve through your purpose, believe in yourself and in your purpose. The devil takes no pleasure in the pursuit of your God-given purpose. Your commitment to God's plan for your life must therefore be girded with faith. Believe in God and in your purpose.

Believing in your purpose will encourage and empower you to succeed in the face of fierce challenges.

> *Whatever I have, wherever I am, I can make it through anything in the One who makes me who I am.*
>
> — PHILIPPIANS 4:13 (MSG)

It takes faith in your purpose to translate your potentials into values that will impact the lives of people around or in your world. Against all odds believe, even if others do not. God's wiring to fulfil your purpose is in you and not others. Hence, whether they believe in your purpose or not should not deter you from fulfilling it. Purposeless life is a meaningless life, therefore until you discover the specific purpose and work it out; you cannot get to the place God has designed for you. Discovering the purpose generates a rich tapestry of experience for yourself and others. It is therefore important that you discover your specific assignment. Stop wandering about, stop imitating people but rather be yourself. Discover your purpose to propel your success, satisfaction and fulfilment in life.

> *Make a careful exploration of who you are and the work you have been given, and then sink yourself into that. Don't be impressed with yourself. Don't compare yourself with others.*
>
> — GALATIANS 6:4 (MSG)

You shouldn't feel sorry to any of your family members, friends or the people around you for wanting to explore God's purpose for your life. Rather, encourage them to explore theirs and you will have a potential partner on the journey to self-discovery. Therefore, stop waiting on other people to give you permission to do what God already appointed you to do. Your life is your own, don't waste it trying to be what others expect. Take full responsibility for your own life and be in the driver's seat because it is your action that ultimately determines your destiny.

Don't hinge finding fulfilment and satisfaction in your life on anybody. You have to be yourself. That is the reason why discovering life-purpose is the key to finding fulfilment and satisfaction in life.

Having a sense of purpose for your life will drive you towards living a life full of satisfaction and fulfilment. Though the early stages of exploration and discovery may often be filled with lots of uncertainty but do not stop, explore more and more to have amazing discoveries. You will never have the motivation to live a fulfilled life unless you know that God has chosen you for a specific purpose, so dig deep.

I believe strongly that God made you for a purpose but to give up on that purpose will amount to contempt.

The only person that can stop the actualization of God's purpose for your life is you. The devil cannot stop you if you do not stop yourself. All of his antics to stop will amount to nothing. Do not be the clog in the wheel of the actualization of your own purpose.

God chose you, called you His child, created you for a specific purpose precisely at this time and precisely at this location.

~

And He made from one man every nation of mankind to live on all the face of the earth, having determined their appointed times and the boundaries of their habitation.

Acts 17:26 (NASB)

CHAPTER 2

YOUR ADAPTATION PLACE

You have the capacity to be fulfilled wherever you are, changing your location may not be necessary.

Every tree or plant is found in the locality where the conditions which favour its growth exist. One tree grows best in the sheltered valley, another by the water's edge, another on the bleak mountain top swept by the storms while some require full exposure to the sun for their optimum growth. There is adaptation in nature.

As plants have their ecological adaptation, God places us in a place with peculiar circumstances and experiences where our lives will grow and ripen the best. The peculiar circumstances to which we are subjected are the experiences we all need to bring out in us the beauties and glamour destined for us by God.

The place where you find yourself might be the place God desires you to live your life and impact the world around you. Your place of birth is not by accident but part of the factors that will contribute to the fulfilment of your life's purpose.

A little fable tells of a primrose growing by itself in a shady corner of the garden which became discontented as it saw the other flowers in their mirthful beds in the sunshine, and begged to be moved to a more conspicuous place. Its prayer was granted. The gardener transplanted it to a more showy and sunny spot. It was greatly pleased but there came a change over it immediately. Its blossoms lost much of their beauty and became pale and sickly. The hot sun caused it to faint and whither. So it prayed again to be taken back to its old place in the shade.

As the wise gardener knows best where to plant each of the flowers, God knows where His children will best grow into what He would have them become. There is a place where God set as your own space to live, fulfil purpose and impact the world around you.

God chose you, called you His child, created you for a specific purpose precisely at this time and precisely at this location. You are in the right place. You may have to work extra hard to succeed because of the instability in government policies and harsh economic situations yet God knows what is best for you and where best your purpose will thrive. He makes no mistakes. In this regard, changing location may not be the right step as you have the capacity to be fulfilled wherever you are. Changing your geographical location may not change your resource allocation because it is fixed by God.

> *From one man he made every nation of men, that they should inhabit the whole earth; and he determined the times set for them and the exact places where they should live.*
>
> — ACTS 17:26 (NIV)

Don't run away from the place where God set for you as your own space, where your portion is kept and left for you, all because life in that territory is harsh, difficult and full of challenges.

To fulfil your life's purpose and live a beautiful Christian life, you should be willing and ready to submit to various kinds of discipline and be encouraged when facing all manners of difficulties and challenges, cropping up at the place where God set for you to live.

So, it becomes much safer to purposely navigate your own course of life rather than passively living each moment to chance and environmental factors. Every aspect of your life is somehow a result of your creation. It depends on what you do with your life in whatever place you find yourself. Learn to always take advantage of the opportunities springing up in your location at every given time—No one will harness them for you.

Whatever our life is to be, beautiful or marred, fulfilled or unfulfilled we must make it just where we are. It is now up to you to create a life that is impactful on the world around you. No restless discontent can change your lot, if you are not pushed over by the prevalent conditions in your environment. "Do what you can with what you have, where you are" [1], remarked Theodore Roosevelt.

BEAUTIFUL ANYWHERE

> " *. . . Lo I am with you always"*
>
> — MATHEW 28:20

Since there is no place, the presence of God cannot penetrate and no terrain His grace cannot infiltrate, the power of God can come to play whether at the wilderness or at the desert and the light of God can shine through the darkness of obscurity. He can use the weak things to confound the strong and the foolish the wise. God's grace can be made available to man at the lowest place of the earth; no matter where you are, His grace can always be available to you.

> *And God is able to make all grace abound to you . . .*
>
> — 2 CORINTHIANS 9:8A (NIV)

God did not mistakenly place you in the place you find yourself per time. He places you at the location where your purpose can best thrive in advancing your life's purpose. Hence, the place of your birth, the colour of your skin and the situation you find yourself and some other things about you are in line with the purpose of God for your life. Here's a quick check. He will provide for all your needs wherever you are only if He's the One that brought you there. You may not have to leave the wilderness to a more comfortable zone before you actually live a purposeful life.

I have made up my mind not to seek greener pastures anywhere because God's grace and wisdom can make the grasses on my side greener. Since God did not make mistake on my skin colour, race and my place of birth, I believe where God put me is in line with His purpose for my life. He created me and put me in a place where I will better fit into the purpose for which He made me.

> *And He made from one, every nation of mankind to live on all the face of the earth,*

having determined their appointed times, and the boundaries of their habitation."[2]

You too can make up your mind to stay where God puts you per time and ensure your purpose comes through. You do not necessarily need to change your location before you can fulfil that purpose you have been destined for.

Government's policies can be bad (creating more wealth for the rich and making the poor more impoverished); the nation's economy may be too harsh, even the people may be bad. All these should not misdirect your purpose because God's plan does not depend on a nation's economy or the people in the nation.

Since God does not work by the environment and circumstance but according to His divine purpose, God's grace will be allotted to you in your place, so that His divine purpose will come to play in your life. Though the world is full of sufferings it is also full of beauties, and life can be awesome and beautiful for you even at your own place too.

In this respect, do not underrate any forms of experience emanating in your place. Each is a potential key to unlock the potentials and treasures in you and speed you up for fulfilment.

The condition of life in the place you meet yourself should therefore not deter you, but rather propel you to develop a philosophy that if others are fulfilling life's purpose where they are, you too will. Doing this will make you believe that life can also be beautiful at your place. Once you first believe this, you are well disposed to taking positive actions in the direction of your belief. This will help you focus on God and your purpose. Therefore, take your focus off your circumstances and put it on God.

Daniel fulfilled purpose in Babylon and Joseph too in Egypt. Times were unfavourable and their place of location seemed very hostile; yet they kept their focus on God and on fulfilling their life's purpose. The Lord can see you through every trying time. The more the trials become fierce, the more of divine grace that is supplied by Christ. There is therefore no environment of trial characterised by difficulties or hardship in which you cannot live a fulfilled life. Whatever the social or environmental factor, your economic standing, status or educational attainment, the assurance is that you will fulfil your purpose at the place God puts you. You only need to believe in your purpose and leverage on God's abundant grace available to you.

GRACE THROUGH FAITH

All of God's provisions, grace inclusive flow to individuals through the energy of faith. God has not provided an alternative way to access His provisions and grace, it comes through faith. Faith is therefore the key that connects man to divine grace.

> *"...we have gained access by faith into this grace..."*
>
> — ROMANS 5:2 (NIV)

The power of faith supplies sufficient quantities of the grace of God into your life to empower you to fulfil your God-given purpose, where others are falling victim of devil's antics.

Without the presence of God and His divine grace, it will be difficult to navigate life varied experiences without getting disconnected from life-purpose. Therefore it is obvious you need faith to experience His divine presence and grace wherever you find yourself.

It is important that you continue in faith to enjoy constant supplies of grace on a daily basis, so that you will not get drowned in life challenging situations.

Grace is available anywhere you find yourself, you only need to connect it through faith in God because it is the only basis through which you can receive divine grace.

GET DETERMINED

Many Christians have given room to the devil to kill their life's purpose using the deadly spiritual weapon of discouragement. Many have failed in achieving their life's purpose owing to failure to persist in the pursuit of their life's purpose especially in the face of trials, difficulties, challenges and unpleasant circumstances of life.

One major reason for this is the feeling of discouragement. Feeling discouraged is enough to make life tiring and uninspiring, frustrating and defeated. It also disconnects man completely from his life-purpose as man shifts his focus away from God to focusing on the magnitude of his difficulties and challenges. As a way out of this trap, when you are discouraged locate people that will inspire you to get up and get going. This will help you avoid getting disconnected from focusing on God and your purpose. It is wise not to dwell among aimless people because they will infect you with the wandering spirit.

> *Walk with the wise and become wise, associate with fools and get in trouble.*
>
> — PROVERBS 13:20 (NLT)

A resolve to be determined is one of the wisdom you need to actualize your main reason on the planet earth. Determination fuels the drive in you to keep you going towards the actualization of the purpose sets aside for you by God.

When you are determined, nothing can stop you from fulfilling your purpose. Not even the devil can because *'there is no chance, no destiny, no fate that can hinder or control the firm resolve of a determined soul'* – Ela Wheeler Wilcox.[3] Developing the spirit of determination eliminates quitting out of the options you have. It builds in you the drive to keep going in spite of the roadblocks and setbacks. Therefore do not just wait for the situation and circumstances to change, but be resolute to make things happen positively.

There will be a way when there is a will. Determination also produces the will to fight on in the face of challenges confronting you. The most important thing you need to fulfil that specific assignment designated to you by God and affect the world around you is determination, because

> *Determination can accomplish almost anything, and in this lies the great distinction between the great men and little men.*[4]
>
> — THOMAS FULLER

It is interesting to note that

> *"Death is not the greatest loss in life. The greatest loss is what dies inside of us while we are still alive."*[5]
>
> — NORMAN COUSINS

So when the drive to pursue your life-purpose dies in you, life becomes pointless, purposeless and non-impactful.

Dear friends, be resolute never to give up with life because the devil will try to play-up the card of bad conditions of the place you find yourself with the view to making fear and frustration set in, deter you and to make you resign to fate.

By the power in the precious blood of Jesus Christ, I frustrate every antics of the devil that makes you throw in the towel in the pursuit of your life-purpose; hindering you from actualizing your purpose, so that your life will radiate the glory and beauty of God. I release on you the strength and determination to win the battle against the devices of the devil that make life purposeless and not worth living. Amen.

Lucius Annaeus Senecca quips,

> *"Rough road leads to the heights of greatness.*[6]

Therefore, make up your mind that you will settle for nothing less than the actualization of that particular purpose God designed for you. Never take "No" for an answer. God won't let the circumstances stop your purpose. Get on with the pursuit of your life-purpose wherever you find yourself, bearing in mind that a determined person makes a significant difference and a small group of determined people can change the course of history.

The tests, trials and tribulations of your life are purposed by God so that you may achieve divine potential

—John Hagee

~

Dear brothers and sisters, when troubles come your way, consider it an opportunity for great joy. For you know that when your faith is tested, your endurance has a chance to grow.

James 1:2-3 (NLT)

CHAPTER 3

THE TRYING MOMENT

And we know that in all things God works for the good of those who love him who have beencalled according to his purpose — **Romans 8:28 (NIV)**

We all hope to have a problems-free and tribulation-free journey on the way to fulfilling our life-purpose and in the Christian race generally, but this might not be so because there are troubles and tribulations that will test our faith and patience and prove us ready for the blessings God will bestow upon us in life.

Though there will be periods of relative peace, no one will be exempted from the trials of life. Different people with different kinds of trials, no one can be completely exempted. While some have a greater number of afflictions, some have fewer trials. Every man regardless of skin colour, age, income level or place of birth will pass through different kinds of trials to get to the peak of his life.

Some of the trials that come our way are as a result of our errors and disobedience. While some trials come as a result of man's disobedience and error, some trials come from God to draw us closer to Himself and get us ready for the blessing He will release on us. The suffering of Job is referred to as

> “*all the trouble the Lord had brought upon him*”
>
> —JOB 42:11 NIV

But the joy is that we will not be tried beyond our ability.

> “*There hath no temptation taken you but such as is common to man, but God is faithful who will not suffer you to be tempted above that ye are able . . .*
>
> — 1 CORINTHIANS 10:13

Trials come in the form of hardship, difficulties and affliction. Through these trials we grow in the direction of maturity so that, at whatever situation we find ourselves, we will not lose focus on our life-purpose, as we would have grown in our perseverance level and built a degree of resilience against the devil and the world that want to destroy our purpose in order to make life miserable for us.

> *Consider it pure joy, my brothers whenever you face trials of many kinds Because you know that testing of your faith develops perseverance*
>
> — JAMES 1:2-3 (NIV)

> *Dear friends, don't be surprised at the fiery trials you are going through, as if something strange were happening to you. Instead, be very glad . . .*
>
> — 1 PETER 4:12-13 (NLT)

> *And not only so, but we glory in tribulations also: knowing that tribulation worketh patience;*
>
> *And patience, experience; and experience, hope: And hope maketh not ashamed; because the love of God is shed abroad in our*

hearts by the Holy Ghost which is given unto us.

— ROMANS 5:3-5

Patience in this passage could also be translated as "perseverance" or "endurance" while the word experience means "tested" or "proven character". Tribulation is valuable to us because it teaches us to persevere and not to give up. As we persevere under trials we develop strong character and unshakable hope.

Trial helps produce endurance and when we endure we have the willingness to accept whatever comes, determined to stand firm, have insight to see God in all of our circumstances and enjoy His provisions. Through endurance, we earn an increasingly perfect result that makes us more mature in Jesus Christ because trial itself plays an indispensable role in bringing us to maturity. God uses trial to refine, strengthen and keep us from falling.

"*The tests, trials and tribulations of your life are purposed by God so that you may achieve divine potential*"[1]

— JOHN HAGEE

And in achieving divine potential you fulfil God's specific assignment for your life.

In line with the scripture in Romans 8:28,

> "*And we know that in all things God works for the good of those who love him, who have been called according to his purpose*"

God uses the circumstance of life both positive and negative in the environment to shape us to the image of His dear Son and fit for His purpose for our lives. It may be difficult to exonerate ourselves from trials, so we should take solace that the Lord can use every trial to help us become more like Jesus Christ and fit for our purpose.

> "*Perseverance must finish its work so that you may be mature and complete not lacking anything*
>
> — JAMES 1:4 (NIV)

You might have been rejected by family members and friends or cursed but know that you are in the right place. God puts you in the middle of fiery trials to burn out the imperfections and craft you into a vessel that will bring glory to His name and impact the world around you positively.

One of the tactics of the devil is to try to make us believe that we are alone in our trying moments, so that we can give up when we feel lonely in our difficult situation. He has successfully made some Christians to turn back from pursuing their life-purpose because they thought that the trials they are passing through is because God has abandoned them. Some even abandoned their faith and turned to the other side of the divide. They forget the trial is ultimately for their own purpose. Rather than accusing God of abandoning you, you need to inquire of the Lord — *Lord, in what way are you using this trial to make me become more like you?* In the appropriate time, the Lord will answer your inquiry.

The truth is that God has not abandoned you. Going by His promise,

> “*I will never leave thee nor forsake thee*”
>
> — HEBREWS 13:5

He will not abandon you during your trying moments. Therefore when the “feeling” of His presence is missing, always have the assurance that the Lord is with you both in the good times and the bad. Only that you bear in mind He is using the trials to burn out the imperfections, shape you to the image of His dear Son and make you fit for His purpose. So whatever trouble in this life a child of God meets with is all the hell he will ever have, there exists an almighty, all-wise, infinitely gracious and sovereign God who knows about them.

It is worrisome how Christians who are supposed to impact the world around them through their life's purpose fail to know that God knows everything about their trials. As such, they derailed from God's purpose because they fall victim to the circumstances they find themselves in. They were trapped by the corruption and ungodliness in the society and lost the beauties of Christ in their lives. They throw in the mud, their Christian fidelity and holy conduct because they cannot endure their trying moments. They could neither maintain Christian faith nor remain focused in the pursuit of their life-purpose.

These societal vices (corruption, lust, ungodliness and lots more) are some of the temptations that tend to derail believers on their paths to fulfilling their divine purpose. These vices are the forces a believer must fight against to fulfil his life-purpose. No matter how tense our trying moments are, we must remain focused to win the battles of the enemy to make our lives worthless.

JOB'S TRIAL

Job was a man that remained focused during his trying moment. He went through a great trial and tribulation, which included the destruction of his properties, the death of his children and loss of his health. The scriptures gave a vivid description of Job's trial;

> "*And there came a messenger unto Job, and said, the oxen were plowing and the asses feeding beside them; and the Sebeans fell upon them, and took them away; yea they have slain the servants with the edge of the sword, and I only am escaped alone to tell thee.*
>
> *While he was yet speaking, there came also another and said, the fire of God is fallen from heaven, and hath burned up the sheep, and the servants and consumed them, and I only am escaped alone to tell thee.*
>
> *While he was yet speaking, there came also another, and said. The Chaldeans made out three bands, and fell upon the camels, and have carried them away. Yea, and slain the servants with the edge of the sword, and I only am escaped alone to tell thee.*
>
> *While he was yet speaking, there came also another and said, Thy sons and thy daughters were eating and drinking wine in their eldest brother's house*

And, behold, there came a great wind from the wilderness, and smote the four corners of the house and it fell upon the young men, and they are dead and I only am escaped alone to tell thee.

—JOB 1:14-19

In all these things, Job did not sin by charging God with wrongdoing, neither did he have the thought that God has abandoned him –

> "*in all this Job sinned not, nor charged God foolishly*
>
> —JOB 1:22

When his wife and friends advised him to deny God for abandoning him, he responded and said,

> "*Though he slay me, yet will I trust in him, but I will maintain my own ways before him"*
>
> —JOB 13:15

Job could see at the end that his trying moment is ultimately for his own purpose. He found great comfort, wisdom and plan of God; to the point that he said,

“*I have heard of thee by the hearing of the ear, but now mine eye seeth thee*”

—JOB 42:5

Life can be so cruel, but there is a degree of grace awaiting your grab so that you can endure and wait on God while the trial is ushering in testimonies for you.

You don't get stronger by taking the easy way out. You grow stronger during difficult times. Like Job, believers must be ready to endure trials to attain divine destiny. See each difficulty and hardship period as a leverage to grow stronger in faith. Instead of allowing your trials to hinder you, you should be humble enough to learn spiritual lessons from them, to be able to live a purpose driven life and a beautiful Christian life. It is an exercise in futility to pray that trial will not come your way rather pray for the strength to go through it in order to come out shining and to rejoice in trials because they awaken your awareness of God's closeness to you in the midst of your circumstances.

ENDURE TRIALS

The soldier who runs to the rear when the battle is fierce is not a hero, he is a coward. True victory is not found in escaping trials, but in rightly enduring and facing them. Trials strengthen Christian's faith and make them grow stronger to face the challenges that crop up in the Christian journey and in the quest to fulfil purpose. If you cannot endure trials, you will never get the testimonies that come after. The man who goes through trials is the next God promotes.

Escaping trial may lead to abandoning of the original purpose for your life and pursuing shadows. And by this, you will not be able to impact the world as God has planned for you by assigning a particular purpose through which you should affect the world positively. And when you abandon your life purpose, you become a wanderer—aiming towards nothing in life.

The best men the world ever reared were brought up in the school of adversity and hardship. Adversity is always the partner of any worthwhile achievement. It tests your quality. It is the refiner's fire that burns out the impurity and helps you reach your maximum potential. Every difficult situation should therefore nerve us with fresh determination to win and come out shining as these trials refine and bring out the best in us. No man can emerge a hero without fighting a battle.

Recognizing that adversity is always the partner of any worthwhile achievement will put you in the right frame of mind while facing the heat of adversities. Anytime you embark on any worthwhile achievement, expect trials in the form of problems, difficulties or obstacles.

To endure trials, we have to acknowledge the hand of God in our trying moments. If we refuse to acknowledge His hand in our troubles and difficulties, we may abandon our faith and run to the other side of the divide when the trials become fierce and seem unbearable. Christians must accept that God can use their hardship to bless them and make the world a beautiful place to live. Accepting this fact boosts a believer's confidence that

> *"weeping may last through the night, but joy comes with the morning"*
>
> — PSALM 30:5B NLT

Trusting in the Lord is another anchor on which trials turn to testimonies besides acknowledging the hand of God in our trying moments. Though all your prayers return unanswered from the still white realm above and all things seem upside-down and sorrows fall like rain and troubles swarm like bees about a hive, believe and trust God,

> *"casting all your cares upon Him, for He cares for you"*
>
> — 1 PETER 5:7 NKJV

You really need a trusting heart to move on while you experience trials, if not, you are most likely to give up on life. Trust the faithfulness of God to see you through. Trust in His unfailing love for divine sustenance. And your cry should be,

> “*in you I trust o my God. Do not let me be put to shame nor let my enemies triumph over me*”
>
> — PSALM 25:2 NIV

Do not be embittered, consider your trials as pure joy and continue trusting in the unfailing saving power of the Almighty for your trials to turn to testimonies and your hardship to a pleasant situation because God has great things waiting for you on the other side of the dark day. Turn and begin to trust Jesus Christ, *“a friend who sticks closer than a brother”* (Proverb 18:24b NIV). He will not abandon you in all fierce trying moments of yours. He will be by your side and see you through.

> “*Consider it a sheer gift, friends, when tests and challenges come at you from all sides.*
>
> — JAMES 1:2 (MSG)

As you are trusting God for your trials to turn to testimonies, learn to speak God's word back to Him in prayer. Praying God's word back to Him assures you that you are guaranteed a listening audience at the throne of grace. Always go to God's word to see what it says and base your prayer on the promises of God. Praying God's promises revives your courage to continue waiting on Him, assures you of God's abiding presence, His power to sustain you and His provisions for all your needs during your trying moments.

> *Now this is the confidence that we have in Him, that if we ask anything according to His will, He hears us. And if we know that He hears us, whatever we ask, we know that we have the petitions that we have asked of Him.*
>
> — 1 JOHN 5:14-15 (NKJV)

> *Let us therefore come boldly to the throne of grace, that we may obtain mercy and find grace to help in time of need.*
>
> — HEBREWS 4:16 (NKJV)

The person who is strong in the word will be strong in faith and the person who couples that strength in the word with his or her praying will be a victorious person in the face of fierce trials. Be versed in the word so that you can be strong in faith and your faith can be an overcoming faith.

Though you have a choice to endure or escape trials, note that there is no victory for the man that escapes difficulties and tribulations which come along with success stories and life fulfilment. Those who fight on and vigorously pursue their life-purpose without looking back assuredly will have victory. You are not alone in the struggle; God is on your side. The tribulations and hardship will roll by and your life will radiate the beauties and glamour of God.

> *The most common trait I have found in all successful people is that they have conquered the temptation to give up*".[2]
>
> — PETER LOWE

Do not give up in your trying moments because after the trials come testimonies.

Big obstacles and insurmountable roadblocks can be removed by a mustard seed kind of faith. It is what we need to change the verdict when life sentences us to hardship. Your success in your trying moments depends on your faith. Be strong in faith, be determined and resolute that the purpose of God for your life will come through anywhere you find yourself; whether at the desert, or at the wilderness or at the spring of water.

Keep believing in Him, never give up. Believe in the hand that never fails and daily pour out your requests to Him, because His hand is not shortened that it cannot save, neither His ear heavy that He cannot hear (Isaiah 59:1). The answer to your prayers will come and the bright shining day shall appear for you. Only resolve in your mind that whether at the desert or at the spring of water, life can be beautiful for you.

You cannot arrive at your life's purpose by starting with a focus on yourself. You must begin with God your Creator

— Rick Warren

~

For everything, absolutely everything, above and below, visible and invisible, rank after rank after rank of angels — everything got started in him and finds its purpose in him.

Colossians 1:16 (MSG)

CHAPTER 4

FULFILLING PURPOSE

Unless you assume a God, the question of life's purpose is meaningless.

— Bertrand Russell, atheist

You will never find the satisfaction and fulfilment you desire in life until you tap into your purpose to fulfil it.

Just as the coming of Jesus Christ to this world and paying the price for man's sin was established before the foundation of the world, your life purpose has been established before you are born into this world. God knew it before the foundation of the world was laid. Hence, it cannot be changed. The world is therefore waiting for your arrival. It is waiting for you to fulfil all that has been purposed for you, because the world will miss your assigned experience or purpose if you fail to live it.

Your purpose equals your calling. It is something you are set aside to fulfil. It is not something you can earn, God purposed it for you. It is part of your makeup, which makes you valuable to the world around you. You will never find the satisfaction and fulfilment you desire in life until you tap into your purpose to fulfil it.

Your purpose is part of the grace of God in your life. In order to enjoy the fullness of that grace that has been unleashed on you in terms of your natural gifts, you have to embrace your purpose. You will achieve the highest degree of meaning in life only by embracing God's purpose for your life. Consider this illustration. Many years ago, a meeting of very high net worth individuals was held where it was decided that someone must be appointed and empowered to resolve certain matters affecting their businesses negatively. All preparations were made both to train and deploy the appointed messenger. The messenger's main purpose is to solve all business challenges and doing differently will never satisfy or fulfil his purpose. The messenger in this illustration is you and God is the One who has appointed and prepared you well both for training and deployment in our world – His business firm. Fulfilling your purpose is therefore fulfilling your functions and your functions are the supernatural abilities you have to offer to the world.

Fulfilling your purpose will not only take you into the depths of yourself, it will guide you along the journey to being the real you—you will not just follow people. You will also have a wealth of insight which you may never have tapped into before. This helps you with goal setting, refining and nurturing your life-goals until your purpose is fulfilled.

A number of people right from a tender age know what exactly they will do in life, while some others do not even consider their life-purpose until they clock thirty to forty. Unfortunately, some others go to the grave never realising what their life was all about. Which class of people do you belong to? Those that discover theirs early, late or those that go to the grave wondering why they were on earth.

You may wonder why some people get special attention or get things done in an easier way. The secrets of this set of people is that they pay close attention to everything around them, responding enthusiastically to the positive things that come their way, maximising the negative ones, having a clear idea about who they are and what they want to do with their lives, time and energy.

Nobody is luckier to get attention than the other person in life. Your reaction to the issues of life and your purpose perspective strongly determine the satisfaction and fulfilment you get. There is no magic about this. It is all about the way you see life and react to it.

CHRIST: THE PLATFORM FOR FULFILMENT

Rick Warren, writing on "It all starts with God" writes;

> the search for the purpose of life has puzzled people for thousands of years. That's because we typically begin at the wrong starting point – ourselves. [1]

You cannot arrive at your life's purpose by looking outside God because He is the One that created you and He alone knows the purpose assigned to you. You must begin with God, your Creator, because

> *unless you assume a God, the question of life's purpose is meaningless"* [2]
>
> — BERTRAND RUSSEL

It is only in Him you can discover your purpose. Every other thing you look up to cannot give you the clue on your life purpose. To discover your purpose and fulfil it, you must turn to God.

> *For everything, absolutely everything above and below, visible and invisible everything*

got started in him and finds it purpose in him

— COLOSSIANS 1:16 (MSG)

In Ephesians 1:11-12 (MSG), Apostle Paul wrote to the church at Ephesus that it is only in Christ that they can find life purpose – who they are and what they are to live for.

> “*It's in Christ that we find out who we are and what we are living for. Long before we first heard of Christ and got our hopes up, he had his eye on us, had designs on us for glorious living, part of the overall purpose he is working out in everything and everyone.*

For the reason that you did not create yourself, there is no way you can dig out what you were created for by yourself. There is therefore the need for you to seek God until He begins to enlighten you on what your purpose is. This will take some work and patience on your part, so you have to painstakingly work and wait patiently on God. Let God show you the purpose He assigned to you. You might not get the whole picture at once but as you open your heart little by little, He will unfold it to you.

> *If people can't see what God is doing, they stumble all over themselves; But when they attend to what he reveals, they are most blessed.*
>
> — PROVERBS 29:18 (MSG)

The fulfilment of life's purpose is available to all who believe in Christ Jesus but we will never find true fulfilment when we choose desires that are outside of that purpose. Only a life that is surrendered to God enjoys true fulfilment, so that His plan might be worked out in us, we need to believe in Him and surrender to His will.

Strength and skills are never enough to fulfil your purpose. The right platform to fulfil your purpose is Christ alone—on the platform of His grace. Jesus Christ is the only true anchor on which the fulfilment of life's purpose is possible. The journey into fulfilling life-purpose therefore begins with genuine conversion. It is after you are saved that you step into divine purpose.

Paul stepped into divine purpose after his encounter with Jesus Christ on his way to Damascus to persecute Christians. It was said of him,

> *. . . This man is my chosen instrument to carry my name before the Gentiles and their*

Kings and before the people of Israel. I will show him how much he must suffer for my name"

— ACTS 9:15-16 (NIV)

After spending some days with the disciples at Damascus, Paul started venturing into his purpose – he started preaching in the synagogues that Jesus is the Son of God. If you want to discover and fulfil your life-purpose, then you must first offer your heart to God in repentance and accept the offer of Salvation.

When you welcome Him into your heart and He becomes your life's travelling companion, He will continually make His purpose about your life known to you. He will open your eyes to see the things He has set in motion for you to be fulfilled in life. Set your heart towards God and delight yourself in Him, He will open your eyes to see deep things and give you the resources including wisdom to chart the course of your life.

Ironically many people will not fulfil their life-purpose because they choose to live without Him on earth. The closer you are to God, the easier you discover the whole essence of your life here on earth and the better you fulfil it.

Our God is ready to give provisions that will help us fulfil our purpose on earth. But one must be in Christ to access these provisions. The person that accepts Jesus Christ as his Lord and personal Saviour has access to the heavenly provisions that can make him actualize his purpose. Such provisions include grace, divine enablement, courage and fresh oil. Whatever things are needed to face the challenges that come along fulfilling purpose are available in sufficient quantities for those in Christ Jesus.

> *Christ gives me the strength to face anything.*
>
> — PHILIPPIANS 4:13 (CEV)

The Message translation reads

> *Whatever I have wherever I am, I can make it through anything in the One who makes me who I am.*

Believers will not be able to impact the world without the anointing of God upon their lives. You need to be anointed by the Holy Spirit so that you can fulfil God's plan for your life. Continually receiving a fresh anointing will equip you to fulfil God's purpose on the earth and be a reservoir of God's glory

> *I shall be anointed with fresh oil*
>
> — PSALM 92:10B

Seek to be anointed with fresh oil on a daily basis by partnering with the Holy Spirit daily because you cannot access the anointing of the Holy Spirit without being filled with the Holy Spirit.

God has provided all the necessary tools to fulfil your purpose and impact the world. He only calls on you to acknowledge His power that can help you to be fulfilled and rest on His grace that grants you divine enablement to launch into things beyond human ability and reasoning.

Therefore, stepping into your purpose will not therefore happen overnight but as you push into fulfilling your God-given purpose, things will begin to work for your good. Those things will continue to work in your favour until all things are working for your good. How much things work for your good will be in direct proportion with how much of your purpose you are fulfilling. Hence, to the degree that you give yourself towards the pursuit of your purpose will be to the degree of impact you make on the world around you, and the degree that this physical world gives itself to your good.

When anything in creation fulfils its purpose, it brings glory to God. For you to impact the world and bring glory to God, come to God through Christ, the truest source of fulfilment in life and think of taking an adventure towards your purpose.

You have no right to anything you have not pursued because the proof of your desire is in the pursuit
— Mike Murdock

~

Whatever turns up, grab it and do it. And heartily! This is your last and only chance at it, for there's neither work to do nor thoughts to think in the company of the dead, where you're most certainly headed.
Ecclesiastes 9:10 (MSG)

CHAPTER 5

TAKE AN ADVENTURE

"If it is going to be, it is up to me."
— Earl Nightingale

~

Striving for a fulfilled life without an adventure is like trying to harvest where you have not planted.

If you are going to fulfil your life-purpose and make life beautiful for yourself anywhere you find yourself, whether at the harsh terrain or the comfortable terrain, it is up to you. Nobody will be blamed for your misfortune. That is why you need to take an adventure to make your purpose come through.

It is not enough to go on prayer and fasting towards actualizing your life-purpose; you have to strike a balance. Whenever you pray and fast and you leave all the responsibilities to God, such prayer and fasting will have no basis (your responsibilities) to become fruitful and will not yield any result. You have the responsibility to turn your life-purpose to reality.

God's instruction to Abraham in Genesis 13:17,

> *"Go walk through the length and breadth of the land, for I am giving it to you"* (NIV)

shows that we cannot achieve life's purpose unless we take at least a step towards it. You really have to work towards your purpose. Stop thinking that everything will fall in line as God has purposed it without a corresponding effort. No, you have to take an adventure towards that purpose you are on the earth for. Striving for a fulfilling life without an adventure is like trying to harvest where you have not planted. Diving into purpose requires launching into an adventure. In this regard, nothing will be more important than using your time, resources and energy to do what you are on earth to do—your life-purpose.

Mike Murdock says,

> *You have no right to anything you have not pursued, because the proof of desire is in the pursuit."*[1]

To exercise your right on any achievement, you will embark on an adventure that will last for the rest of your life and this makes you embrace your life purpose, pursue and fulfil it. Then you will see yourself doing the unbelievable. You will accomplish great things that will impact many lives, all because you yielded to your purpose and ventured into it.

People who are afraid of adventure never actualize their purpose. They dare to fulfil their life-purpose but cannot find the courage to enter into it. These people will never find the true meaning of life and neither can they add value to the world around them. They will never trust God with their lives and wouldn't venture into an opportunity that would spur them into action towards fulfilling their purpose. They will never venture into fulfilling their purpose. Like a lazy person, they are fond of saying;

> *"There's a lion out there! If I go outside, I might be killed!"*
>
> — PROVERBS 22:13 (NLT)

Immediately Apostle Paul discovered his purpose, he took an adventure that empowered him to fulfil what he was cut-out for. He dared authorities, risked his life by going to forbidden places to preach the gospel and turn people to the kingdom of God. He dared the storms and the shipwrecks, all for the sake of positively affecting people around him with his life-purpose. In the quest of fulfilling his purpose no matter what, Apostle Paul stood before King Agrippa to defend God's mission for him, he said.

> *I was not disobedient to the vision from heaven. First to those Damascus, then to those in Jerusalem and in all Judas and to the Gentiles also, I preached that they should repent and turn to God and prove their repentance by their deeds*
>
> — ACTS 26:19-20 (NIV)

Apostle Paul's adventure lasted for the rest of his life. Though he had no idea of where his purpose was going to take him, he lived his purpose fearlessly. He raised the dead and healed the sick, witnessed to kings and brought blessing of comfort to thousands of believers most of whom he led to salvation. As a result of embracing his purpose and giving himself completely to fulfilling it, Paul fulfilled a purpose that continues to speak to us, today. He single-handedly did more to launch the gospel into the non-Jewish world than any other. Besides, he wrote half of the New Testament.

Paul who was called to open the eyes of the Jews and the Gentiles, in order to turn them from darkness to light, and from the power of Satan to God (Acts 26:18) did not fold his hands on his purpose but ventured into fulfilling it. When he looked back over the thirty years of his adventure as an Apostle, he quipped;

> *I have fought the good fight, I have finished the race; I have kept the faith.*
>
> — 2 TIMOTHY 4:7 (NIV)

One can invariably say that what Apostle Paul was saying here is - I have fulfilled purpose; I have impacted the world with my calling by opening the eyes of the Jews and the Gentiles and turning them from darkness to light, and from Satan to God and there awaits me a reward with God.

Thomas Edison was one of the men in the world, who ventured into making an impact on the world. As soon as he got the idea of the light bulb, he started experimenting with his idea to create a light bulb. After thousands of failed attempts, he did not stop on his adventure to create the light bulb. If Edison was not adventurous he would have stopped and given up after so many attempts. Purpose might not be actualized in an easier way, but you have to push on in your quest to fulfil it.

He ventured into many more attempts before he fulfilled his idea of creating a light bulb. He did not mind the cost of fulfilling purpose; all he was about was its actualization in order to leave an imprint in the sand of time.

Thomas Edison quips

> “*Many of life's failures are people who did not realise how close they were to success when they gave up.*”[2]

Attaining your goal in life is all about fulfilling your specific purpose. If you stop before the finishing line of achieving that purpose, then the result will be the same as if you never discovered your purpose or pursued it at all. Don't give up on your life purpose; don't sign off until you actualize it.

Purpose will never translate to physical value unless an adventure is taken towards fulfilling it with a willingness to persist in the face of challenges. If you fail to attempt, you will fail to attain. Until you are willing and ready to take an adventure no compelling reasons will force you.

> *Whatever turns up, grab it and do it. And heartily! This is your last and only chance at it, For there's neither work to do nor thoughts to think In the company of the dead, where you're most certainly headed.*
>
> — ECCLESIASTES 9:10 (MSG)

Are you cut-out for making an impact in the academic world? Take an adventure into academics! Make bold steps towards scaling every stage to assume your call, not minding the risks and challenges involved. No one can stop you, if you do not stop yourself. Therefore, according to Wilfred A. Peterson, you need to take note that

> *Success is focusing the full power of all you are on what you have a burning desire to achieve."*[3]

If I have a purpose to reach the world with the gospel of the Lord Jesus Christ like Apostle Paul, after I might have discovered that purpose, my adventure to fulfilling that purpose of mine include rigorous study of the Bible, Bible dictionary, commentaries and other Christian literatures that give me accurate knowledge of Christ, His kingdom and principles, and getting a platform to dish-out life changing messages to the world around me.

Other adventures I need to undertake will include attending seminars to improve my knowledge on Christian ministry, prayer conferences and partnering with the Holy Spirit to increase my anointing and the level of impact I can achieve by my purpose.

You might have been designed to provide a solution to a particular human need, providing that solution is what actually makes you fulfilled in life. The numbers of cars you have, houses built or children raised are not what make you fulfilled in life. It is the impact you make on the world through your life-purpose. Please, bear this in mind that you are not fulfilled in life if you pass through the world without impacting it positively.

Your adventure is the service you render towards working out your purpose. It sets you on motion to make things happen in your life. Service is the rent you pay for the actualization of your life purpose. It is not something you do in your spare time; it is what you commit the whole of yourself doing in a bid to make yourself relevant to the world. Life can be beautiful if you have the quest to pursue your life purpose and be adventureful towards fulfilling it.

You will really encounter challenges on the road to fulfilling life's purpose. But be inspired by this comment from Winston Churchill:

> "*Success is not final, failure is not fatal; it is the courage to continue that counts.*"[4]

So, the urge for an adventure is what produces the needed courage and determination to forge ahead despite the roadblocks.

Thinking about the resources needed to fulfil that purpose of yours may make you not to sum-up the courage you need to step out on the adventure. Not only would you have realised that there are insufficient resources, but you would have not discovered how to access the available resources. But, if you are bent on discovering the essence of life and venturing into it, you will be amazed at the level of fulfilment you will attain along the way.

That is why you need to encourage yourself and boost your confidence with the scriptures every day you have the opportunity of getting out of bed. Always say to yourself'

> "*I can do all things through Christ, which strengthened me.*
>
> — PHILIPPIANS 4:13

The message version reads;

> *Whatever I have, wherever I am, I can make it through anything in the One who makes me who I am.*

And to your spirit;

> *Be strong and of good courage, and do it, fear not, nor be dismayed for the Lord God, even my God, will be with thee, he will not fail thee nor forsake thee*
>
> — 1 CHRONICLES 28:20

Like Apostle Paul, there can come a time when you can also say that you have fulfilled your purpose and have achieved the reason for your being here on the planet. You can feel fulfilled. You can measure the degree of value you have contributed to the world. But feeling fulfilled does not come on a platter of gold; it comes through services rendered to your purpose. And taking an adventure is the service you pay to make your life impactful, not forgetting that there is time for everything in life under heaven.

Undermining the time factor can be detrimental to the plans that are set to be achieved, even if the plans are rightly set.

~

So watch your step. Use your head. Make the most of every chance you get. These are desperate times!
Ephesians 5:15-16 (MSG)

CHAPTER 6

THE TIME FACTOR

One's best effort towards fulfilling his life-purpose can fail miserably, if exerted at the wrong moment

There is a time for everything and a season for every activity under the heaven; A time to be born and a time to die, a time to plant and a time to uproot
— Ecclesiastes 3:1-2 (NIV)

Ecclesiastes 3:1-8 presupposes that there is an appropriate time for everything under heaven. And when you miss the timing, you may lose it forever since there is no winding back of time. Undermining the time factor can be detrimental to the plans that are set to be achieved, even if the plans are rightly set.

A person's best and well-articulated effort on fulfilling life purpose can fail merely because he acted at the wrong moments. You can do the right thing at the wrong time and miss your destiny. That is why man's effort must match with the time for it to be productive.

Time is a crucial factor to a fulfilled life, and no one with aspirations for a fulfilled life can afford to play with time as it is the very essence of life. Whatever you do with it determines the quality of life and the level of impact you are able to make.

You may fail to utilise your opportunity if you fail to recognize the timing of your purpose. Success and fulfilment are achieved when preparation (the time factor) meets with the opportunity that comes in one's life-time.

Rather than waiting for a bigger opportunity, make the best of the time and opportunity that are available. Jump as quickly as possible at opportunity as it appears because you don't know when another one will set up for you. Stop waiting for an opportunity that may never come.

> “*I returned and saw under the sun, that the race is not to the swift, nor the battle to the strong, neither yet bread to the wise, nor yet the riches to men of understanding, nor yet*

favour to men of skill; but time and chance happeneth to them all.

— ECCLESIASTES 9:11

Satan tempts us to do nothing fruitful with our life; Even busy but doing nothing. The devil understands that time is the real asset of a believer. For this reason he does everything to interrupt the time of believers with unworthy activities in order to make their life pointless, insignificant, unfruitful and unfulfilling. You will be a victim of many things if you don't know how to curb Satan's interruption and redeem the time.

Understanding and redeeming time is about being proactive towards the actualisation of one's purpose in life and willingness to do the right thing at the right time with the right attitude and attention.

Successful and fulfilled people are therefore those that recognize time and use the available opportunity for worthwhile achievements. Unfulfilled people on the other hand fail to understand that opportunity comes, but once. They leave things to chance and are controlled by circumstances and environmental factors.

People who take a long view on life purpose always make better decisions on their time in relation to the issue of life purpose and have a more fulfilled life than people who wait for things to happen. In view of your life purpose and the time factor, you need to take a long view on your purpose in line with the available time. It will help you to make better decisions of your time and activities, do away with unworthy activities clamouring for your attention at the detriment of more crucial activities that would add value to your aspiration on purposeful life.

> *. . . So be smart and learn what to do and when to do it.*
>
> — ECCLESIASTES 8:5B (CEV)

Jesus said,

> *I must work the work of him that sent me while it is day, the night cometh when no man can work."* [1]

This underscores the importance of timing both in human endeavours and God's work. The "day" is the appropriate time you have to take an adventure towards fulfilling your life purpose in order to impact the world, not the "night" because no man can work during this period of time.

The "day" is the active period of your life while the "night" is the time you have become inactive and the law of diminishing return has set in. That a seventy-year-old man is working as a gateman in a company is an indication of how he used his "day". Rather than talking continually about what you are going to do, concentrate on embarking on an adventure now, in the active period of your life to get your purpose fulfilled. Do not wait until the active period of your life is gone before considering doing something meaningful with your life. If you could not recognize the proper time and the principles guiding time, your effort will not yield no matter how hard you press on your efforts towards fulfilling your life-purpose.

> *Because to every purpose there is time and judgment.*
>
> — ECCLESIASTES 8:6

Imagine a man who is supposed to be a world-renowned Evangelist, but neglected and failed to consider how to work towards fulfilling his purpose until he turned eighty. It is not a curse; he is not going to achieve that purpose of his life—for the reason of acting at the wrong moment. No matter how anointed he might be, he is not going to actualize that purpose set aside for him by the Supreme Being. This is because the "day"—his active period is gone and it is impossible for him to store, stop or retrieve time. One's best effort towards fulfilling his life-purpose can fail miserably, if exerted at the wrong moment.

> “*To everything there is a season, and a time to every purpose under the heaven*
>
> *A time to cast away stones, and a time to gather stones together; a time to embrace, and a time to refrain from embracing.*
>
> — ECCLESIASTES 3:1, 5

After the gift of life from God, time is the second most precious gift God has given to man. If you desire to be fulfilled in life, have respect for time and adhere strictly to the principles guiding time. Time management starts with self-management and personal discipline. Therefore learn the art of

> “*making the most of every opportunity because the days are evil*”
>
> — EPHESIANS 5:16 (NIV)

The good news is that the faster you recognize the set time and principles guiding the time, the faster you move, the more energy you have, the more experience you get and the more you learn. The more things you get done and the more you are fulfilled in life.

One of the simplest and yet most powerful ways to get yourself started is to repeat the words,

> *"Do it now! Do it now! Do it now!"*[2]

over and over to yourself according to Brian Tracy. Consider taking the adventure now, do not defer it, do not suspend it. Just do it now. Give it all the push required and you will find things falling in line as God has purposed it for you. Therefore,

> *Whatever turns up, grab it and do it. And heartily! This is your last and only chance at it, For there's neither work to do nor thoughts to think In the company of the dead, where you're most certainly headed"*
>
> — ECCLESIASTES 9:10 (MSG)

STOP SQUANDERING TIME

Life is really short. Even if you were to live for one hundred years or one thousand years, you could not lose any other life than the one you have now and there will be no other life after it on the earth. Both one hundred years and one thousand years are the same considering it as a life span. The most important issue is how impactful such life is. The difference between one hundred years and one thousand years is simply the level of impact made while on earth.

No one can lose the past or the future because they do not belong to him. The time that is gone is gone forever, so the present moment is all you have to either make life fulfilled or unfulfilled, successful or unsuccessful.

> *Redeeming the time, because the days are evil*
>
> — EPHESIANS 5:16

Myles Munroe says,

> *He who has time to burn will never give the world much light. Killing time is not murder, it is suicide.* [3]

Time wasting is suicidal because time wasted is life wasted. Then,

> *Do not squander time for that is the stuff that life is made of.* [4]
>
> — BENJAMIN FRANKLIN

Time will definitely pass away but how much purpose you will fulfil is largely a matter of how your preparation meets with the available opportunities.

> *Don't waste your time on useless work, mere busywork, the barren pursuits of darkness. Expose these things for the sham they are"*
>
> — EPHESIANS 5:11 (MSG)

Beloved, you have a destiny to fulfil. You have an assignment to accomplish. You have a purpose with which you impact the world around you positively. Do not waste your valuable time on something that is neither worthwhile nor moving you towards the fulfilment of your purpose, because anything worthless that takes your time is chopping off part of your destiny.

BE WISE

> *. . . and the wise heart will know the proper time and procedure.*
>
> — ECCLESIASTES 8:5B (NIV)

You have heard it said many times before now that wisdom is the principal thing. Through wisdom, man can set plans and the right time for the plans to come to actualization.

> *Wisdom is supreme; therefore get wisdom. Though it cost all you have, get understanding.*
>
> — PROVERBS 4:7 (NIV)

Wisdom actually gets us acquainted with the fact that time is the basic currency of life which must be used judiciously. Wisdom helps us to discover that time is more valuable than money and that time cannot be stored, stopped or retrieved. Prioritising time is simply wisdom and wisdom is simply appropriating your time for an adventure that makes life valuable, impactful, beautiful and purposeful.

Wisdom will not allow you to go to sleep with your God-given potential. With the right dose of wisdom, you will not mix with the idle people who will initiate you into the gang of the slothful and infect you with the wandering spirit. It will help you locate people that will serve as a catalyst to your life purpose. Do not hesitate to

> *Esteem her and she will exalt you; embrace her, and she will honour you.* [5]

As honey from the comb will be sweet to your taste, so is wisdom to your soul, hence ensure that you find it.

> *Know also that wisdom is sweet to your soul;*
> *if you find it, there is a future hope for you*
> *and your hope will not be cut off.*
>
> — PROVERBS 24:14 (NIV)

To get this wisdom you must subject your mind to the word of God. Study it to get knowledge, meditate on it to get understanding and practise it to get the wisdom that is far above rubies. The rod you need to stir your mind to wisdom is the word of God. Little wonder you need to study the word of God on a daily basis to get the required dose of wisdom for daily endeavours.

> *Get wisdom, get understanding; forget it not; neither decline from the words of my mouth.*
>
> — PROVERBS 4:5

The foolish person can neither strategize nor prioritise his time. This makes him miss the opportunity that comes his way because there is no wisdom to recognize and utilise such opportunity.

> *The fool folds his hands and ruins himself.* [6]

There is then the need for you to be wise to be able to prioritise and strategize the available time to utilise opportunities you have and make yourself valuable to the world around you.

From birth to the time of the final departure from the earth, our lives are counted in seconds, minutes, hours, days, weeks, months and years. Whatever you do with your time will tell at the end of time. The joy is that God will not allow sudden death to take you away. You will fulfil your entire divine mandate. Be wise enough to appropriate your time on adventures that last for the rest of your life, add value to your life, the world and the generation yet unborn.

Whatever life delivers to you depends on the choice you take. You have to choose to succeed or fail, be fulfilled or unfulfilled.

~

Today I have given you the choice between life and death, between blessings and curses. Now I call on heaven and earth to witness the choice you make...

Deuteronomy 30:19 (NLT)

CHAPTER 7

IT'S YOUR CHOICE

You have been engineered for fulfilment from birth but the choices you make determine what happens to you.

~

Life is a sum of all your choices.
— **Albert Camus**

Society sees fulfilment as raising children, having a big job, earning a huge amount of money, building magnificent houses and driving luxurious cars. This is not necessarily true. You can have all these things but if you have not achieved the specific purpose designated to you by God, you are still unfulfilled in life.

The man who measures fulfilment in life by the standpoint of money, houses built, and cars bought has not caught the true meaning of fulfilment because

> *a man's life does not consist in the abundance of his possessions.* [1]

No amount of material possession will give you a sense of fulfilment or make you fulfilled in life. Material possession is not an indicator of a fulfilled life. Don't build your fulfilment in life on the acquisition of material things because life is not defined by what you have, even when you have a lot.

Fulfilment is achieving what is set aside for you by God. It is based on impact made through life purpose. For those called to the drama ministry, their fulfilment is simply in how many lives they impacted through their calling. For those given the talent of singing, their fulfilment is in how much they are able to positively affect lives. For the evangelist, it is in how many lives that have turned to the Kingdom of God—not how many gospel vans were bought or cathedrals built by funds raised in revivals and crusade programmes.

A man can be fulfilled at the wrong things. He may be fulfilled at being lazy, wasting opportunities and not taking charge of his life. Nothing just happens. As fulfilment has to be worked at, unfulfillment equally has to be worked at.

A school of thought believes that *what will be, will be.* On the contrary the law of cause and effect applies to everything in life. What you sow is what you reap (Galatians 6:7). If you sow the seed of indolence, you will reap the fruit of indolence. It is as simple as that. So as it takes effort to be fulfilled likewise it takes effort to be unfulfilled in life.

The law of cause and effect applies to both fulfilment and fulfilment. The unfulfilled person fails to plan, avoids taking an adventure, give-in to trials and folds his hands at opportunities. Your ability to choose, decide and then take an action will determine everything that will happen to you in life.

> *Life is a sum of all your choices.* [2]
>
> — ALBERT CAMUS

In your choices lie the quality of your lifestyle and the level of impact you are able to make on the world around you. You are therefore the sum total of the choices you make and continue to make on a daily basis.

Discovering your specific purpose is taking one step towards fulfilling life purpose but making the right choice opens doors for its fulfilment. Purpose is assigned to you by God, but fulfilment must be earned by you. And if earned, calculated steps must be taken towards fulfilling it.

Fulfilled people have common attributes. They take choices and do not leave things to chance. They are not afraid of challenges and are not stopped by obstacles. They are sensitive to time and are not frivolous about time, thereby maximising time and opportunities. Their faith is greater than their fear. They are optimistic and resolute.

Purpose is therefore not a matter of chance. It is a matter of choice, it is not a thing to be waited for, it is a thing to plunge into in order to achieve it. You will have to be willing to live a fulfilled life because fulfilment is possible for anyone who is willing to achieve it. There is a clear difference between *"wanting to"* and *"willing to". "Wanting to"* stops at the face of challenges, *"willing to"* crosses over the obstacles, while the *'doing'* attitude achieves the set goals and desires. Rather than wanting to, cultivate the willing attitude and transcend to the doing attitude. Be action oriented; the key to reaching high levels of fulfilment is for you to develop the *"doing"* attitude. Discipline yourself to do it immediately and then persist until you have completed it. Therefore,

> " *Love not sleep...* "[3]

If you are observant, you will discover that the person who fulfils life's purpose is the one who discovers his purpose and takes the choice to aim for it unwaveringly. It may seem hard but he does not consider it as humanly impossible. It may seem humanly impossible but he sees the power of God turning it to possibility. Anything humanly possible is within his reach. He goes for the adventure that will make life impactful, fulfilled and beautiful. Things that will make you fulfilled are also within your reach, make the choice to go for it because everything you will need in life to bless your generation and fulfil your life purpose was made available before you arrived.

You will have to choose to succeed or fail, be fulfilled or unfulfilled. Nobody will make the choice for you. Therefore whatever life delivers to you depends on what choices you make. Circumstances and environmental factors will not be blamed for not fulfilling your life purpose. Then you have to be determined to go ahead despite the obstacles that lay before you. Take the choice to turn challenges to prospects for your purpose to thrive. Choose not to be discouraged by the environmental factors. Taking these choices is what will make the difference for you because by your choices, decision and determination, nothing will stop you.

In view of this, you will have to train your mind not to see obstacles on your path as barriers. If you do, you will stop trying and you will not be fulfilled because you will let go of every opportunity that comes your way. See the obstacles as hurdles you can leap over to attain life fulfilment. You have been engineered for fulfilment from birth; accept the responsibility of taking choices in life and dedicate yourself to fulfilling your purpose.

> "*Today I have given you the choice between life and death, between blessings and curses. Now I call on heaven and earth to witness the choice you make...*
>
> — DEUTERONOMY 30:19-20 (NLT)

As life and death are placed before every man to choose from, fulfilled life or unfulfilled life is equally waiting for your choices. Choose to go after your purpose because everything that makes life beautiful is embedded therein.

Beloved it is not the years in your life that count, it is the life in the years that actually counts. So, it is not enough to have lived, you should be determined to live for something because life is quantified on the degree of the physical impact it has made on the physical world. How well you live your life is in the amount of impact you have made in life. Success or failure, beautiful or marred, fulfilled or unfulfilled—all these are determined by the choices we make. The choice to live a fulfilled life or unfulfilled life therefore lies before you. Whatever you choose is what you will have. You cannot choose to only sleep and have a harvest in the harvest time. It is impossible, not even God can help you out when it comes to that. Live your life towards fulfilling the purpose for which you are on the earth and life will be beautiful for you.

Say to God,

> " *Inspire and empower me to take the choice to go for an adventure that will make me to be fulfilled in life and glorify your name in the land of the living as well as impact the world through my purpose.* "

Amen.

Welcome to the path of fulfilment.

NOTES

CHAPTER ONE: NOTHING JUST HAPPENS

1. Rick Warren, *The Purpose Driven Life, (Oasis International Ltd, 1770 S. Randall Road, Geneva, USA, 2002), 23*

CHAPTER TWO: YOUR ADAPTATION PLACE

1. John .C. Maxwell, *Talent is Never Enough, (Nashville, Tennessee Thomas Nelson Inc., 2006), 146*
2. Acts 17:26, *NASB*
3. Inspirational quotes, *https://www.-passiton.com>4218*
4. *My Book*

5. John .C. Maxwell, *Talent is Never Enough, (Nashville, Tennessee Thomas Nelson Inc., 2006), 39*
6. Brainy Quote, *https://www.brainquote.com/quotes/lucius_anneaus-seneca_125252*

CHAPTER THREE: THE TRYING MOMENT

1. John Hagee, *Life's Challenges, Your Opportunities, (The Charisma House, 600 Rinehart Road, Lake Merry, Florida, 2009), 41*
2. John .C. Maxwell, *Talent is Never Enough, (Nashville, Tennessee Thomas Nelson Inc., 2006), 119*

CHAPTER FOUR: FULFILLING PURPOSE

1. Rick Warren, *The Purpose Driven Life, (Oasis International Ltd, 1770 S. Randall Road, Geneva, USA, 2002), 17*
2. *Ibid, 17*

CHAPTER FIVE: TAKE AN ADVENTURE

1. Mike Murdock, *Wisdom For Winning, (Wisdom Publications Inc., Somewille, MA, United States, 1998)*
2. John .C. Maxwell, *Talent is Never Enough, (Nashville, Tennessee Thomas Nelson Inc., 2006), 131*
3. AwakenTheGreatnessWithin, *https://www.awakenthegreatnesswithin.com/accessed*
4. *https://www.winstonchurchill.org/publications/finest-hour-136/media-matters*

CHAPTER SIX: THE TIME FACTOR

1. John 9:4, *KJV*
2. Brian Tracy, *Eat That Frog!, (Joint Heirs Publications Nigeria Limited, Benin City Nigeria, 2001), 103*
3. Myles Munroe, *In Pursuit Of Purpose, (Destiny Image Inc., Shippensburg, PA, United States, 1992)*
4. Benjamin Franklin's Famous Quotes, *https://www.fi.edu>famous-quote*
5. Proverbs 4:8, *NIV*
6. Ecclesiastes 4:5, *NIV*

CHAPTER SEVEN: IT'S YOUR CHOICE

1. Luke 12:15, *NIV*
2. *https://www.bartleby.com/easy/Life-Is-A-Sum-Of-All-Your-PK4D3J3E2LMQW*
3. Proverbs 20:13

ABOUT THE BOOK

You are created to live a life with meaning and purpose, equipped with potentials and designed for a destiny. As a matter of fact, until you discover your personal reason; your specific assignment, you will never be fulfilled in life. It is tragic to be alive and not know the reason why.

Everything that makes life beautiful is embedded in your life's purpose. You can make your life beautiful in any place you find yourself by discovering your purpose and pursuing it with every breath in you.

This book brings together in one volume, important and practical steps on how to figure out 'one thing' you are made for, vigorously pursue your life's purpose with God's specification, fight on in the face of fierce trials of life and make life beautiful for yourself.

The book is easy-to-read, and will enlighten, strengthen and fire you up for the pursuit of your life's purpose in making life beautiful at your place.

ABOUT THE AUTHOR

Oduntan Adebuga is a writer and journalist who has authored some titles that include ***Empowered For Wealth and Fruitfulness.*** He is a senior staff reporter with a news publication in Lagos, Nigeria. He holds a Masters' Degree and Bachelor's Degree in Mass Communication from University of Lagos, Akoka, Nigeria. He is married to Abosede.

www.ingramcontent.com/pod-product-compliance
Lightning Source LLC
LaVergne TN
LVHW091025150826
845672LV00006BA/1690